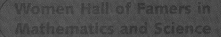
Chien-Shiung Wu

Pioneering Physicist and
Atomic Researcher

Chien-Shiung Wu

Pioneering Physicist and
Atomic Researcher

**Stephanie H.
Cooperman**

the rosen publishing group's
rosen
central

This book is dedicated to Ilene S. Cooperman, the flower in the desert who always believed in me.

Published in 2004 by The Rosen Publishing Group, Inc.
29 East 21st Street, New York, NY 10010

Library of Congress Cataloging-in-Publication Data

Cooperman, Stephanie.
Chien-Shiung Wu : pioneering physicist and atomic researcher/ by Stephanie Cooperman. — 1st ed.
   p. cm. — (Women hall of famers in mathematics and science)
Summary: Explores the work of Chien-Shiung Wu, a physicist and atomic researcher, and examines the hardships she endured to reach the top of her field.
Includes bibliographical references and index.
ISBN 0-8239-3875-1 (lib. bdg.)
1. Wu, C. S. (Chien-shiung), 1912– —Juvenile literature.
2. Physicists—United States—Biography—Juvenile literature.
[1. Wu, C. S. (Chien-shiung), 1912– . 2. Physicists. 3. Women—Biography.]
I. Title. II. Series.
QC16.W785C66 2003
530'.092—dc21
[B]

2002009628

Manufactured in the United States of America

Contents

Introduction

In order to grow, flowers need a few basic things. Flowers need plenty of light and soil rich in nutrients. They also need water and enough room to spread out their leaves. If their needs are met, flowers will grow tall and their blooms will be very full. Sometimes, however, flowers are placed in a pot in a very dark room. They may put down roots in the desert where there is not enough water. Or they may be planted too close to other flowers—so close that their leaves cannot stretch out. In these unfavorable conditions, only the very strongest plants will survive and become beautiful flowers.

The human mind is very much like a flower. It requires certain things in order to reach its fullest potential. People need access to books and good teachers, encouragement from loved ones, and enough room to spread out and discover new things. Some people don't grow up under these conditions, though. They may not be able to go to school. They may be told they cannot have a certain job because of their gender or race. Or they may be discouraged from having new ideas because their thoughts are different from the popular ideas of the time. If people are met with these kinds of problems, they will behave just like flowers. Only the very strongest will accomplish great goals when faced with great obstacles.

Chien-Shiung Wu, the famous physicist, was like a flower in the desert. She grew up in a time and place when women were discouraged from studying math and science. But she didn't let that stop her from chasing her dreams. Even though she struggled to find the right school, the right teachers, and the right career, Chien-Shiung was able to spread her leaves. Determined to succeed, she broke new ground for women in the sciences.

Chien-Shiung Wu's father believed that women had as much right as men to be well educated, and he passed that foresight onto his daughter. She chose to study physics, a difficult subject that intrigued her and that she had to teach herself during the summer vacation before college. She came to the United States to find a better graduate school. She found a career in physics that brought her much success. She tackled some of the toughest questions in physics—questions other scientists thought were too difficult to test. Her many accomplishments include helping to disprove a major law of physics. Although she did not receive a Nobel Prize, which many people thought she deserved, she worked hard throughout her lifetime. She left a legacy of persistence and courage that gave future scientists new drive to do their best no matter what obstacles lay before them.

Chien-Shiung Wu encountered hardships along her journey because she was different from other physicists. First, she was a woman in what was considered to be a man's field of study. Second, she was an Asian person who wanted to study in the United States. Chien-Shiung considered herself to be part of something greater than one gender and one race, but not everyone was as open-minded as she was. Her strength and vision enabled her to grow in a hostile environment, just like a flower in the desert. Her story is a tale of the power of the human spirit. Her work is the creation of a mind in full bloom.

1

Planting the Seeds in China

Chien-Shiung Wu was born on May 31, 1912, in Shanghai, China. Her family, which included her mother and father, two brothers, and a sister, lived in a small town called Liuhe about thirty miles from Shanghai. Just before Chien-Shiung Wu was born, China's government was not a democracy like that of the United States, where representatives are voted into power by citizens and given the power to make laws. Rather, rulers were born into a dynasty. The ruling dynasty at the time was called the Manchu dynasty. In this system, one family is in power and their power is maintained for many years. Wu Zhongyi, Chien-Shiung's father, did not believe this was right. Just a year before his daughter Chien-Shiung was born, he quit engineering school and became a revolutionary, a person who fights for political or social change. He participated in the Chinese Revolution of 1911, which successfully ended the Manchu dynasty and changed the government of China forever.

At that time, women in China were not treated as equals to men. They were taught at home instead of in a school. They had to bind their feet, even though doing so was very painful. Foot binding ensured that a woman would have small feet, a trait that was considered more desirable for women in Chinese culture. But Chien-Shiung's father did not believe women should be treated differently than men. He thought that women should learn as much as men, as was common in other parts of the world. Chien-Shiung's father brought his revolutionary ideas into his home.

FIRST CHANCE AT AN EDUCATION

Wu Zhongyi made sure his sons and daughters were properly educated. In order to give girls like

Chien-Shiung the same opportunities as boys, he opened a school for girls and served as its principal. Since her father's school was the first of its kind in the region, Chien-Shiung was very excited. She studied hard, returning each day to her family's home invigorated from the day's lessons.

The Wu house was not especially large, but the shelves were always lined with books. Magazines and newspapers spilled over the tables. Chien-Shiung's father encouraged her and her brothers to be inquisitive and to read many things. Chien-Shiung became very close with her father and took his advice. She graduated from her father's school when she was nine years old. This was a great accomplishment for a young girl in Liuhe because very few girls went to school—even an elementary school like her father's. But Chien-Shiung wanted to continue to learn. Unfortunately, there were no other schools near her home.

THE NEXT STEP

Chien-Shiung turned to her father for advice. According to *Nobel Prize Women in Science*, by

Sharon B. McGrayne, he would often tell her to "Ignore the obstacles . . . Just put your head down and keep walking forward." The only option for Chien-Shiung to continue her education was to go to a boarding school. There was a good girls' boarding school in Suzhou, fifty miles from where they lived. Together with her family, Chien-Shiung decided this was the best place for her, although it was so far away. This was one of the first obstacles she would have to overcome to continue her education.

The school in Suzhou was called the Soochow Girls' School. It was very much like schools in the United States. The same subjects were taught there as in the United States. Some American professors even came to teach the eager students as guest lecturers. Since they lived at the boarding school, Chien-Shiung and her classmates only saw their families on school breaks. But Chien-Shiung learned to stay close with her family even if she couldn't see them every day. This was a skill Chien-Shiung would use throughout her life, especially when she moved away from China years later.

Chien-Shiung was born in Shanghai, China, pictured here in 1925. Shanghai is located about thirty miles from Liuhe, where Chien-Shiung spent her childhood.

In 1922, Chien-Shiung began high school at the Soochow Girls' School. The school was divided into two parts. One part of the school taught a wide range of academic subjects, including math and science. The other part of the school trained women to become teachers. Chien-Shiung chose to be trained to become a teacher because the tuition for that school was free, and she was guaranteed to get a job after graduation. Chien-Shiung soon found, however, that she missed learning about science. Although she learned many interesting things at school during the day, she craved more scientific knowledge.

A THIRST FOR LEARNING

Chien-Shiung wasn't about to give up her love of learning or desire to know more about science. The girls from both schools lived together in the same dormitory. Chien-Shiung had friends in the academic school. She began borrowing her friends' textbooks in the evening. As the other girls slept, Chien-Shiung would stay up late, studying into the wee hours of the morning. By studying this way, she gained an education from both schools. She paid particular attention to math and science—subjects that she did not learn in her school.

Chien-Shiung's late-night study sessions changed the way she viewed the world. She fell in love with physics (the study of energy, matter, and motion). Her father advised her to enroll in a class at the Soochow Girls' School taught by Dr. Hu Shi, who was known for revolutionizing the Chinese language and introducing its modern form. A brilliant man, Hu Shi saw a special spark in Chien-Shiung and became her mentor. He encouraged her to attend a national university.

Chien-Shiung graduated from the Soochow Girls' School in 1930 at the top of her class. It was no surprise that she gained admittance to the National Central University in Nanjing. She desperately wanted to study physics there. She didn't think, however, that she knew enough to get into the program.

NO STRANGER TO HARD WORK

Chien-Shiung's father wouldn't let her give up on her dream. He knew his daughter needed to study more math and science to be able to excel in the physics program at the university. But he also felt his daughter could learn enough in time to be able to keep up in classes. He brought her math, chemistry, and physics books so she could study over the summer break. Remembering her study sessions late at night, she poured over the books all summer long. Chien-Shiung was finally able to study physics at the National Central University. "Wu's achievement had to be attributed to her father in part, because he was an exceptional man for his day, with very progressive ideas. He could not bear the outdated perception that women had to stay home to be wives or mothers. Rather, he encouraged Chien-Shiung to pursue her studies and to fulfill her dream overseas," Chiang Tsai-chien, science editorial writer for the *China Times*, was quoted as saying in the *Taipei Times* on August 16, 2000.

Chien-Shiung was influenced by her father in other ways. She inherited his persistence and revolutionary tendencies. She had led her high school's chapter of China's underground student movement and represented her classmates at strikes, protests, and meetings. She continued these activities at the university. World War II had not yet begun, but Japan had already threatened to invade China. Chien-Shiung and many of her classmates were

Throughout her life Chien-Shiung worked tirelessly. Her hard work in the classroom eventually benefited a whole new generation of students when she taught at Columbia University. Here, Chien-Shiung sits in her office at Columbia, where she began teaching after World War II.

nationalists, and they believed the Chinese government should stand up against Japan. They organized boycotts of Japanese goods and protested outside the homes of government officials. Once, Chien-Shiung even led a protest outside the president of China's mansion. She had learned from her father to stand up for what she believed in, and that by voicing her opinions and concerns, she could make a difference.

COMING TO AMERICA

When Chien-Shiung graduated from college, she taught physics and performed scientific research. The seeds of knowledge planted during her early years of schooling still required more nourishment. But China did not have any graduate schools where she could continue to study physics. During the two years after college, Chien-Shiung met other educated women. Some had advanced degrees from American universities and recommended that she go to the United States to learn more. Chien-Shiung knew she would have to go to the United States in order to study physics again.

Going to the United States was not an easy thing for Chien-Shiung to do. She had spent time away from her family at boarding school and college. Sometimes she didn't see her parents and siblings for many months at a time. But she had not been as far away as the United States. In addition, getting there and attending school would be very expensive.

Luckily, Chien-Shiung's father was not the only person who believed in his daughter's dreams of becoming a physicist. She had an uncle who also believed in advanced education. He had studied in Europe and returned to China to start the country's first long-distance bus company. He was an entrepreneur, a person who takes the risk of starting a business, and he was a very wealthy man. Since he saw the same good qualities in his niece that Chien-Shiung's father did, he offered to pay for her trip to the United States.

Chien-Shiung's family had confidence in her. They believed she would do great things if given the opportunity. Chien-Shiung had already managed to learn math and science at an advanced level. According to *Nobel Prize Women in Science*, Chien-Shiung said, "If it hadn't been for my father's encouragement, I would be teaching grade school somewhere in China now."

Chien-Shiung left China and her family in 1936 when she was twenty-four years old. She headed to the University of Michigan to earn a Ph.D. in physics. She boarded a ship with all her belongings to take the next step in her incredible journey.

What she didn't know was that she would never make it to the University of Michigan. And the good-byes she gave her brothers, sister, and parents before leaving China would mark the last time she saw her family again.

2

Putting Down Roots in America

When she arrived in San Francisco, California, Chien-Shiung's plans changed entirely. She met Luke Yuan (formerly Chia-liu Yuan), a physics student at the University of California at Berkeley. Luke came from a very well known family in China. His grandfather was a famous general who was elected the first president of the Republic of China. But Luke's grandfather tried to use his power to create his own dynasty.

Luke's father believed in democracy just like Chien-Shiung's father. He disagreed with Luke's grandfather's attempts to pass power down through their family. Luke's father had to go into exile because he had defied

As a young girl in China, Chien-Shiung was encouraged to get a good education. Her desire to learn took her to the University of California at Berkeley, where she began advanced studies in physics, a field she would eventually become well known in.

Luke's grandfather. Children were supposed to respect their elders in China and not question their authority. With his father gone, Luke was left alone with his mother. The family could no longer benefit from the grandfather's wealth and they became poor.

Like Chien-Shiung, Luke loved studying science, especially physics. He knew he would have to travel to the United States to attend graduate school. He chose the University of California at Berkeley because some of the best minds in physics were already studying and working there. Chien-Shiung visited Berkeley to learn about their physics program. She was just as impressed by the talented professors as Luke was. When she met Luke, who was already a student at Berkeley, she cemented her decision not to continue on to Michigan. Professors at that school often poked fun at Chien-Shiung later, saying she stayed in California because of Luke. The two did fall in love, but Chien-Shiung never admitted to them whether or not that was why she had stayed.

WORKNG WITH THE BEST

While at Berkeley, Luke and Chien-Shiung studied under some of the greatest physicists in the world. They were taught by Ernest Lawrence, a man who went on to win a Nobel Prize for his work with the cyclotron. The cyclotron was a machine that smashed atoms together at very high speeds. They also learned how atoms and parts of the atom, called subatomic particles, behaved in different conditions. Another one of their well-respected instructors, Robert Oppenheimer, achieved fame when he went on to lead the Manhattan Project— the United States's project that produced the first

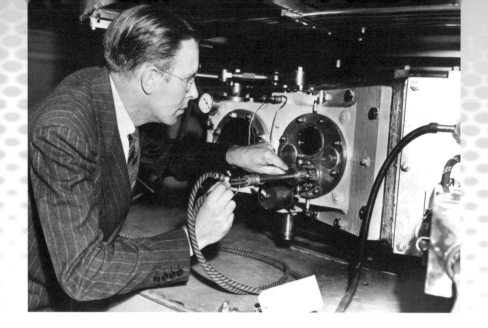

Ernest Lawrence is pictured here with his cyclotron. His work with this machine led to him winning the Nobel Prize in 1939. Chien-Shiung had the privilege of working closely with him while she attended school in Berkeley.

atomic bomb during World War II. Chien-Shiung and Luke would learn many things about atoms, including how they can be used for both constructive and destructive purposes.

Chien-Shiung became interested in nuclear physics while at Berkeley. Nuclear physics is the study of the nucleus of the atom. Chien-Shiung was intrigued by the smallest subatomic particles. Ernest Lawrence headed Berkeley's physics department.

Robert Oppenheimer graced the cover of Time *magazine on November 8, 1948. He led the Manhattan Project, the United States's building of an atomic bomb, and became well known for his efforts.*

He had an assistant named Emilio Segré. Chien-Shiung joined Segré's team and began her studies into the complicated world of atoms. Segré was known for his quick temper, but he treated Chien-Shiung like a family member and expected her to do great things.

Working very hard in the lab, Chien-Shiung became known for putting in long hours. She would often have to be told to go home. Robert Wilson, who was also a graduate student at the time, told biographer Sharon Bertsch McGrayne in an interview that he would ride by the lab in his jalopy and say, "It's time to go home, Miss Wu." The pair would ride

ALL ABOUT ATOMS

What is an atom? Everything in the universe is made of atoms. Atoms are the building blocks of matter. They have a center, called a nucleus. The nucleus is made of two kinds of particles, called protons and neutrons. Protons are positively charged and neutrons have no charge at all. Outside of the nucleus are electrons. These are particles with a negative charge. The electrons create the "shell" of the atom.

There are smaller particles than neutrons, protons, and electrons. Nuclear chemists and physicists use accelerators to break down atoms to discover very tiny pieces of matter. These are called subatomic particles, and scientists started discovering them in the 1950s.

How do atoms bond together to create matter? Atoms like to have their shells filled with a certain amount of electrons. Some atoms have too many electrons. These atoms look to give their electrons to atoms that don't have their shells filled, and they bond together. Some atoms have too few electrons. They look for atoms that have electrons to share. Then they bond together. In this way, the shells of both atoms are filled.

home together. Chien-Shiung took her education very seriously. Little did she know that she was studying under a future Nobel Prize winner—an honor she would come close to receiving herself.

A DIFFERENT WORLD

Chien-Shiung missed her family and the way of life she left behind in China. Everything was different and new to her in the United States. People dressed differently, ate different foods, and spoke a different language than she was used to. Chien-Shiung learned to speak English long before she got to Berkeley. But she chose to wear her traditional Chinese dress and eat Chinese food. After just one visit to the Berkeley cafeteria, Chien-Shiung decided she'd have to find some other place to eat.

It was in a local bakery in 1936 that Chien-Shiung met Ursula Schaefer, another graduate student. They became instant friends. Ursula Schaefer was from Germany and didn't like the school's cafeteria either. They would often eat together and teach each other about their cultures. They found a great way to eat Chinese food for very little money: There was a Chinese caterer near their school who would let them eat banquet leftovers for only a quarter. Luke would often join them. Ursula always thought of Chien-Shiung as "an absolutely, totally reliable friend," according to *Nobel Prize Women in Science*, and the pair stayed close for over fifty years.

Many people at Berkeley thought Chien-Shiung was very beautiful. People noticed her beautiful smile. She also drew attention because of the way she dressed. Chien-Shiung ordered her clothing from China or Taiwan and continued to dress traditionally throughout her life, never conforming to the style adopted by most Americans.

NEWS FROM HOME

Chien-Shiung took comfort in her friendship with Ursula and her relationship with Luke. But food and clothing weren't the only things different in the United States. Chien-Shiung lived in the

While studying at Berkeley, Chien-Shiung lived in the International House, pictured here. At this dormitory, Chien-Shiung met other students from around the world.

International House, a dormitory for students from all over the world. Although the United States would not enter World War II until years later, battles would soon be fought in Europe and Asia. One morning Chien-Shiung left her room and picked up a newspaper to find some very shocking news: Japan had invaded China, as it had been threatening to do for years.

Chien-Shiung maintained constant contact with her family while in school. But after Japan attacked China, she lost all contact with her parents and siblings. The news from her homeland was very disturbing. She read newspapers describing Japanese victories in many Chinese cities, including Shanghai, which was very close to her family's home. Chien-Shiung worried about her family's safety. Caring people at the university tried to calm her fears. Two Japanese students even left flowers on her bed to express their sympathy.

Chien-Shiung studied even harder after the battles began in China. She knew she could

At the University of California at Berkeley Chien-Shiung worked closely with some of the most well known physicists in the world, such as Emilio Segré (left) and Robert Oppenheimer (middle). Here in 1940, the three take a break from physics.

not return home, so her progress at the university became even more important. While she couldn't help her family in China, she could continue her father's dream of getting the best education possible.

Chien-Shiung received her Ph.D. from Berkeley in 1940. She stayed at the university for two more years working as a research assistant in the physics department. According to

American Women Scientists by Moira Davison Reynolds, Emilio Segré said he thought the university should have hired Chien-Shiung for full-time status, adding that "they would have had a star." During this time, she studied fission, the process of splitting an atom's nucleus. Just a year earlier, Otto Hahn and Fritz Strassmann, two German chemists, had split the atom using fission. Chien-Shiung quickly became an expert on fission. She gave lectures around the country. According to *Nobel Prize Women in Science*, Robert Oppenheimer sometimes called her "the authority" because she knew so much.

"ASK MISS WU"

Many of Chien-Shiung's fellow students could not pronounce her first name. Instead, they called her "Miss Wu." They did not know that "Chien-Shiung" means "courageous hero" in Chinese, nor could they guess that "Chien-Shiung" would stay true to her name and accomplish so many brave acts.

She became well known throughout the country for her knowledge. Scientists were trying to test nuclear fission at a lab in Hanford, Washington. They wanted the nucleus of the atom to split and continue splitting without any help from outside forces. But after a few hours, the experiment stopped working and no fission took place. Enrico Fermi, the physicist heading the experiment, thought that when the atom's nucleus split, it produced a gas that stopped fission. He was told to "ask Miss Wu." Sure enough, Chien-Shiung had the answer. A gas called xenon was causing the problem; Chien-Shiung had studied it for her Ph.D. thesis. Her solution would later lead to the development of the very weapon that ended World War II—the atom bomb.

Chien-Shiung was quickly becoming famous as an expert in many areas of physics, but the physics department at Berkeley would not hire her. This was not surprising, considering that the United States's most outstanding universities did not hire female physics professors at the time. So even though the male professors at these same universities often asked Chien-Shiung for advice on the experiments they conducted, she was not allowed to have the same professional position that they did.

Chien-Shiung was also the subject of discrimination because she was Chinese. Some Americans distrusted Asians because the Japanese were waging war in another part of the world. Many Japanese were forced to leave their American homes and live in internment camps—places where prisoners of war were kept—until the war was over. Americans were afraid that Japanese individuals might act as spies, although no Japanese were ever convicted of spying. In all over 110,000 people of Japanese descent from the West Coast, most of whom were already U.S. citizens, were forced into camps with other Asians in isolated regions of the country. They were not allowed to leave the camps or have contact with relatives in Japan. Even today it is astounding to think that so many people were denied basic constitutional rights in the United States. Although the Chinese were fighting against the Japanese, some Americans did not distinguish between the two groups.

3

Growing with the War Effort

Many of Chien-Shiung's fellow graduate students went to work for Robert Oppenheimer in a different capacity after he left the university. Oppenheimer was working on creating the first atom bomb in Los Alamos, New Mexico. Since Chien-Shiung was an Asian woman, and therefore subject to discrimination because of her gender and nationality, she was not asked to join the team. She had to find another path to continue her study of physics.

In the summer of 1942, Chien-Shiung had something other than physics on her mind. Her relationship with Luke had progressed and they decided to take a major step: She and Luke got married. The ceremony was held at the home of Robert Millikan, Luke's thesis advisor and winner of the 1923 Nobel Prize in physics.

MOVING EAST

Luke and Chien-Shiung moved to the East Coast after they were married. Luke worked in Princeton, New Jersey, designing radars that would eventually be used to help defeat the Germans in World War II. Smith College, a women's college in Massachusetts, offered Chien-Shiung a teaching position. Unfortunately, Smith College could not afford to let her do the research she longed to do. Instead, she had to concentrate on teaching. The newlyweds lived many miles apart but visited each other at the halfway point in New York City when they could.

Chien-Shiung was unsatisfied with her position in life. She was far away from her husband and could not go to the lab as much as she liked. But opportunities were opening up in the most prestigious American universities. Since

During her time at Smith College in Northampton, Massachusetts, Chien-Shiung focused on teaching. Here in the physics laboratory in 1942, she assembles an electrostatic generator.

many professors were on defense leave to help with the war, universities were in desperate need of science professors. Even though many of these schools would not allow women to be students, they did hire female professors.

In 1943, Chien-Shiung became the first female professor at Princeton University, a school that would not have accepted her had she applied as a student because she was a woman.

CHIEN-SHIUNG WU'S FIRSTS

In addition to becoming the first female professor at Princeton University, Chien-Shiung also racked up a string of other firsts. She was the first woman to receive an honorary doctorate from Princeton University; the first woman to receive the Research Corporation Award; the first woman to receive the Comstock Award from the National Academy of Sciences; the first woman to be elected president of the American Physical Society; the first recipient of the Wolf Prize from the state of Israel; and the first living scientist to have an asteroid named after her.

Nevertheless, she was thrilled to be working in the same city as her husband. She was indirectly involved with the war effort since most of her students were navy officers seeking advanced engineering training. At this time, Chien-Shiung did not know that she would eventually play a much bigger role in the outcome of World War II.

JOINING THE MANHATTAN PROJECT

Little did Chien-Shiung know that she had already helped start the building of the atom bomb when she answered Enrico Fermi's question during his fission experiment. But it was not until she was a Princeton professor that Chien-Shiung was asked to join the Manhattan Project—the United States's effort to build the first atomic bomb.

Although mostly men are credited with this massive achievement in nuclear physics, much of the project's research was done by women. Chien-Shiung Wu was one of the many women who helped build the weapon that would end World War II.

The Manhattan Project had its roots in Europe. In Sweden in 1938, Lisa Meitner and her nephew, Otto Frisch, were examining data from a Berlin laboratory. Meitner had worked in the laboratory until the German government began their persecution of the Jews. On re-examining the data, Meitner realized that something had caused the nucleus of an atom to split. She called the process fission.

Frisch told Niels Bohr, the Danish Nobel Prize winner, about nuclear fission. When Bohr attended the Fifth Washington Conference on Theoretical Physics the next year, he soon realized what a major impact the discovery of nuclear fission would have on the world around them. The energy released when a nucleus split was millions of times greater than the energy released when whole atoms reacted. The physicists at the conference also knew that nuclear fission could be self-sustaining. That is, once a reaction was set off, the nuclei of the atoms would continue to divide. Immense amounts of energy could be released.

RACING FOR THE A-BOMB

Scientists from around the world began developing plans to use nuclear energy as a weapon. The Germans started a program to develop an atomic weapon in 1939. By 1940, the British also had research in place. The Soviet Union had its own program, but the Nazi invasion of 1941 put an end to it. And the French gave Nobel Prize winners Irene Joliot-Curie and her husband, Frederic Joliot, the honor of heading the research in Paris.

In these early years, scientists struggled to understand the very basics of nuclear fission.

THE INCREDIBLE POWER OF NUCLEAR ENERGY

Nuclear energy is the energy released when the nucleus of an atom splits or is fused with another atom's nucleus. Fusion is when two nuclei come together. Fission is when one nucleus is split into two or more parts. Scientists use fission and fusion to create nuclear energy. Chien-Shiung worked with fission and fusion reactions in her research.

Fission is the process of splitting an atom. When this happens, energy is released. Nuclear physicists shoot neutrons at atoms. When a neutron hits the atom's nucleus, the atom wants to split apart. Once the atom splits, neutrons are given off. These neutrons shoot into other atoms. When they hit a nucleus, that atom will also split and give off more neutrons. This process happens over and over again in what scientists call a chain reaction. It's just like pushing one domino in a row of dominoes. Once one atom splits and there are extra neutrons in the area, more atoms will split, too.

Fusion is the process of two nuclei coming together. Scientists use huge machines to make fusion occur. It needs to be very hot for a fusion reaction to happen. Fusion happens on the sun, where temperatures can reach into the millions of degrees. A fusion reaction may be very hot, but it produces much less energy than a fission reaction.

Surprisingly, experimental results were published in literature that could be read by people in other countries, despite the fact that scientists soon realized the awesome power of fission. Countries would soon be in a race to build the first atom bomb.

Physicists in the United States knew that a fission chain reaction was possible. They also knew that once they harnessed this power, they might produce a weapon that would change the nature of war forever. In 1939, Fermi began his work on producing a chain reaction that would release an enormous amount of energy. It was during these experiments that he asked Chien-Shiung for help.

At this time in Europe, the Nazi leader Adolf Hitler was quickly subduing Germany's neighboring countries. The Nazi persecution of Jews had forced many Jewish scientists to flee to the United States. The Hungarian Leo Szilard was one of these physicists. He understood that the possibility of producing a military weapon using nuclear fission was urgent because of the Nazi threat. Szilard and two other Hungarian scientists, Edward Teller and Eugene Wigner, persuaded Albert Einstein, the

Albert Einstein spoke out about the dangers of nuclear weapons. He felt that the United States needed to have the same technology as other nations, some of which had already begun building atomic weapons.

famous physicist who had fled the Nazis and was a top scientist in the United States at the time, to sign a letter to President Franklin Roosevelt. The letter told the president that an atomic weapon was possible and that the Germans might be in the process of making one.

One of Roosevelt's advisors, Alexander Sachs, brought him the letter and convinced him how urgent the matter was. Roosevelt did not waste any time. He appointed a Uranium Advisory Committee. Uranium is the main element used in

Albert Einstein
Old Grove Rd.
Nassau Point
Peconic, Long Island

August 2nd, 1939

F.D. Roosevelt,
President of the United States,
White House
Washington, D.C.

Sir:

Some recent work by E.Fermi and L. Szilard, which has been com-
municated to me in manuscript, leads me to expect that the element uranium may be turned into a new and important source of energy in the immediate future. Certain aspects of the situation which has arisen seem
to call for watchfulness and, if necessary, quick action on the part
of the Administration. I believe therefore that it is my duty to bring
to your attention the following facts and recommendations:

In the course of the last four months it has been made probable -
through the work of Joliot in France as well as Fermi and Szilard in
America - that it may become possible to set up a nuclear chain reaction
in a large mass of uranium,by which vast amounts of power and large quantities of new radium-like elements would be generated. Now it appears
almost certain that this could be achieved in the immediate future.

This new phenomenon would also lead to the construction of bombs,
and it is conceivable - though much less certain - that extremely powerful bombs of a new type may thus be constructed. A single bomb of this
type, carried by boat and exploded in a port, might very well destroy
the whole port together with some of the surrounding territory. However,
such bombs might very well prove to be too heavy for transportation by
air.

*This letter, written by Albert Einstein to President Franklin
Delano Roosevelt, outlines the importance of creating a
committee to research the use of uranium in weapons.*

The United States has only very poor ores of uranium in moderate quantities. There is some good ore in Canada and the former Czechoslovakia, while the most important source of uranium is Belgian Congo.

In view of this situation you may think it desirable to have some permanent contact maintained between the Administration and the group of physicists working on chain reactions in America. One possible way of achieving this might be for you to entrust with this task a person who has your confidence and who could perhaps serve in an inofficial capacity. His task might comprise the following:

a) to approach Government Departments, keep them informed of the further development, and put forward recommendations for Government action, giving particular attention to the problem of securing a supply of uranium ore for the United States;

b) to speed up the experimental work,which is at present being carried on within the limits of the budgets of University laboratories, by providing funds, if such funds be required, through his contacts with private persons who are willing to make contributions for this cause, and perhaps also by obtaining the co-operation of industrial laboratories which have the necessary equipment.

I understand that Germany has actually stopped the sale of uranium from the Czechoslovakian mines which she has taken over. That she should have taken such early action might perhaps be understood on the ground that the son of the German Under-Secretary of State, von Weizsäcker, is attached to the Kaiser-Wilhelm-Institut in Berlin where some of the American work on uranium is now being repeated.

Yours very truly,

A. Einstein

(Albert Einstein)

Einstein explained that this research had already begun in America, but additional funds were needed so that the research could be carried out more quickly and efficiently.

nuclear weapons, such as atomic bombs. It is used to start fission chain reactions. In February 1940, the first funding for the Manhattan Project reached Columbia University in New York City. It was soon learned that Szilard was right. The Germans had indeed begun studying nuclear fission. The Uranium Committee soon became a subcommittee of the National Defense Research Committee. More funding was issued to the Manhattan Project.

In November 1940, the National Defense Research Council gave an additional $40,000 contract to Columbia University. By 1941, sixteen contracts for about $300,000 were awarded to other major universities and professional organizations. The research differed from institution to institution. But the institutions had one common goal: to use nuclear fission to create a weapon the world had never seen before.

A CRITICAL INTERVIEW

The Division of War Research contacted Chien-Shiung at Princeton University in 1944. She went for an interview at Columbia University. Two physicists questioned her extensively about physics all day. Even though the lab's projects were secret, the physicists had forgotten to clean the blackboards in the room. When they asked her if she knew why they had called her there, she pointed to the unwashed boards. The physicists laughed at their error and asked her to start the next day. Chien-Shiung joined a research group led by Harold Urey.

Chien-Shiung's group used a process called diffusion in their work. Diffusion can be explained this way: Atoms, like people, don't like to be crowded. Which would you choose: a bus where you had to stand in the back because there were so many people or an empty bus where you could sit down? You would probably choose the one in which you could sit down. Atoms are the same way. They move from a place that is crowded to a less crowded place. This process is called diffusion. Chien-Shiung's group used this technique to separate uranium. Their laboratory was set up in a converted automobile warehouse near the Columbia campus.

USING THE TECHNOLOGY

By the time Chien-Shiung joined the Manhattan Project, the United States was fighting with the Allied forces in both Europe and Asia. Casualties on both sides were increasing in numbers. Although Germany surrendered in 1944, Japan showed no signs of buckling. President Harry Truman made the decision to use the atom bomb that had been developed during the Manhattan Project. The United States dropped a uranium bomb on the Japanese city of Hiroshima on August 9, 1945. Three days later, the United States dropped a plutonium bomb on Nagasaki, another Japanese city. The Japanese surrendered, and World War II was officially over on September 2, 1945.

Chien-Shiung's research helped to create a weapon, the use of which over fifty years ago continues to influence world politics today. Satisfied that she had returned to research and had aided the Allied victory, Chien-Shiung then turned her attention to her family in China. China had fought Japan longer than any other nation. Luckily,

The uranium bomb was responsible for the destruction of Hiroshima, Japan. The mass destruction is evident in this photo, taken just days after the bomb was dropped. Chien-Shiung's research aided the United States in building this weapon.

Chien-Shiung's parents, brothers, and sister were all doing well. They were able to communicate through letters a few times a year. Her father had become more than a hero in her eyes. He had engineered the Burma Road, a highway 621.4 miles (1,000 kilometers) long built by hand through the Himalaya Mountains between Burma and China. This road help the Allied powers bring supplies to the Chinese army.

CHIEN-SHIUNG WU

Chien-Shiung became one of the few physicists from the Manhattan Project who was asked to stay at Columbia University after the war. She had achieved a goal that had once seemed impossible: a professorship at a university with facilities for research. Her husband worked at Brookhaven National Laboratory on Long Island, New York. Luke and Chien-Shiung welcomed a new addition to their family in 1947 when their son, Vincent Weichen Yuan, was born.

The family lived in an apartment owned by the school just two blocks from Chien-Shiung's laboratory. Chien-Shiung adapted to her new roles as both a physicist and a mother. She hired a caretaker for her son. Years later, Vincent attended a boarding school on Long Island. He and his father would return to the city on Friday afternoons and stay for the weekend. Luke would often meet his wife at her lab and help her students with their research.

4

Springtime for Wu

Even after World War II was over, the aftermath was still being felt throughout the world. As the United States was helping to rebuild parts of Europe and Asia, battles were being fought elsewhere. Communists (a group of people who favored a system of government in which all goods are shared between all the people), led by Chiang Kai-shek, were fighting a civil war in China. China's National Central University offered both Chien-Shiung and Luke jobs and a chance to return to their families. But Chien-Shiung's father told her to stay in the United States because of the unstable political conditions. This was good advice. Chinese scientists who traveled to Communist countries after World War II were often not allowed to return to the United States. Chien-Shiung and Luke decided to become U.S. citizens instead.

Chien-Shiung stayed loyal to her culture. She continued to wear traditional Chinese clothing, eat Chinese food, and keep her Chinese name. Unfortunately, there was a Philadelphia bank fraud officer with the same name, and the Immigration and Naturalization Service thought Chien-Shiung was this man! Columbia University eventually cleared up the problem. Chien-Shiung learned that discrimination against Asians was not always intentional.

A HUGE BREAKTHROUGH

Having made the decision to continue her career in the United States, Chien-Shiung set out to find a research project. Enrico Fermi, the scientist Chien-Shiung had helped with his famous fission experiment, had established a theory on beta decay. Beta decay is a type of radioactivity. Radioactivity is the process by which something gives off rays or particles of energy. In beta decay, an atom's nucleus ejects certain parts and changes into another element.

Fermi predicted how the atom's nucleus would behave during beta decay. His theory proposed that the electrons would come out of the nucleus very fast. Unfortunately, scientists in the United States, England, and Russia had done experiments that opposed his theory. They found that the electrons came out at very slow speeds.

MORE ON RADIOACTIVITY

Radioactivity is when the nucleus of an atom breaks down into smaller particles and energy is released. Three types of particles can be produced after the breakdown occurs. They are called alpha, beta, and gamma. Alpha particles have a positive charge. Beta particles have a negative charge. Gamma particles have no charge. The particles also have increasing levels of energy. Beta particles are faster than alpha particles. Gamma particles are the fastest of all.

Chien-Shiung turned her attention to this problem. She used her lab at Columbia University to devise a series of experiments.

Chien-Shiung discovered the problem. The scientists who had experimented before used materials of uneven thickness. Chien-Shiung found that when she used a radioactive material with the same thickness all around, the electrons traveled at the exact speeds predicted by Fermi. An uneven thickness had caused the electrons traveling through the thick sections to bounce off each other and lose speed.

This was a huge breakthrough in nuclear physics. Other scientists did experiments to see if Chien-Shiung was right. Time and time again they found that a uniform thickness made all the difference. Chien-Shiung's fame and reputation grew as a result. Scientists had long wondered why beta decay occurred the way it did. Chien-Shiung had cleared up a problem in physics that had gone unsolved for many years. By doing so, she allowed scientists to use this knowledge to make many other discoveries involving physics.

In her laboratory at Columbia University, Chien-Shiung helped to prove Enrico Fermi's theory on beta decay. Her findings helped to clarify a major law of physics, and she received a lot of attention for her precise work.

In 1980, Chien-Shiung gathered with other noteworthy physicists, Tsung-Dao Lee (far left), *Emilio Segré* (middle), *Robert Serber* (second from right), *and Gian Carlo Wick* (far right). *All of the scientists pictured here have made significant contributions to physics.*

"Her beta decay work was important for its incredible precision," said California Institute of Technology professor William Fowler, according to *Nobel Prize Women in Science.*

"C. S. Wu was one of the giants of physics. In the field of beta decay, she had no equal," said Tsung-Dao Lee, a Columbia University professor, in the *Columbia University Record* years later.

Many scientists thought Chien-Shiung should have won the Nobel Prize for her work on beta decay. The Nobel Prize for science, however, is given only to a person who makes a new discovery. Chien-Shiung found an answer to a very perplexing question, but it was not a new finding.

PROFESSOR WU

During the late 1940s and early 1950s, Chien-Shiung worked primarily on beta decay. She treated her physics students at Columbia with respect, but she also demanded a lot from them. She expected them to be as excited about physics as she was. Emilio Segré, who had known her from her Berkeley days, called her a "slave driver," according to *Nobel Prize Women in Science*.

One of her graduate students, Noemie Koller, described her as being ". . . never satisfied. She wanted people to work late at night, early in the morning, all day Saturday, all day Sunday, to do things faster, to never take time off," according to *Nobel Prize Women in Science*. She worked her

Chinese students even harder because she knew firsthand about the discrimination Asians faced. On one occasion, Chien-Shiung became upset on a Saturday night when she saw that none of her students were at the laboratory.

Chien-Shiung liked to be very involved with her students' work. Sometimes her students wanted more time alone with their projects. One day they bought Chien-Shiung and Vincent tickets to a movie. But Chien-Shiung had given the tickets away to Vincent and his caretaker, so she would have more time to spend in the classroom. The students were very surprised—and disappointed—when Chien-Shiung entered the classroom unexpectedly that day.

Some of Chien-Shiung's students actually referred to her as the Dragon Lady. The name came from a comic strip called "Terry and the Pirates." In this comic strip, there was a character named the Dragon Lady who was similar to Chiang Kai-shek's wife. They used the name in jest. They knew how much Chien-Shiung wanted them to succeed. She was demanding and did not tolerate laziness, but she also wanted her students to love physics the way she did. And she always remembered the best advice from her father: "Ignore the obstacles . . . just put your head down and keep walking forward." She passed this advice along to her students by expecting their best at all times.

Nevertheless, Chien-Shiung once again felt the familiar pangs of discrimination. She had helped clarify a major problem in physics. She had dedicated herself to her students. She was known throughout the world as one of the great physicists. Yet she was not asked to join the Columbia faculty until 1952—years after she began her research at the university. Chien-Shiung eventually received a privileged position as a tenured professor, but not before she weathered the storm of discrimination against women and had waited a long time.

LEE AND YANG ASK FOR HELP

Having solved the great riddle of beta decay, Chien-Shiung set out to explore other problems.

She found a very interesting one in 1956 when Columbia physicist Tsung-Dao Lee stepped into her office.

"Lee came up to office on the thirteenth floor of Pupin Physics Lab," Chien-Shiung said at the International Conference on the History of Original Ideas and Basic Discoveries in Sicily in 1994. "He asked me a series of questions concerning the status of the experimental knowledge of beta decay. Before T. D. left my office, I asked him whether anyone had any ideas about doing this test . . . I suggested that the best bet would be to use cobalt 60 . . . Dr. Lee was very interested in the possibility of such a strongly polarized cobalt 60 . . . and asked me to lend him a reference book on the method."

In an atom there are protons, neutrons, and electrons. There also may be subatomic particles, or pieces of an atom that exist for only a few seconds during a reaction. Today, almost 200 subatomic particles have been discovered. Subatomic particles were usually found when

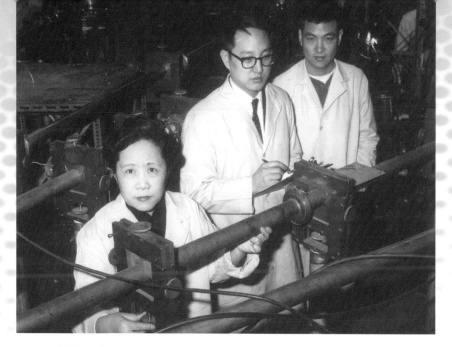

Chien-Shiung, here with Dr. Lee and Dr. Mo in 1963, spent a lot of time in the lab. The scientists conducted studies that led to the confirmation of the theory of conservation of vector current, which was proposed in 1958.

atoms were smashed in accelerators. Lee and his partner Chen Ning Yang were dealing with a new particle called the K-meson.

The K-meson seemed to violate a basic law of physics. The law of parity stated that all molecules, atoms, and nuclei behave symmetrically. That means what happens on one side also happens on the other. But the K-meson did not follow this law. Lee and Yang thought that the law of parity might not apply to the nucleus. They suggested that the nucleus might be right- or left-handed and favor one direction over another. When the electrons came out of the nucleus during a reaction they went one way or the other. The law of parity was proven by many mathematical equations. Since 1925, scientists had accepted the law of parity as fact in all types of interactions. The idea that it might not be entirely correct was not even considered. That is, until Yang and Lee came along.

Scientists had long thought that when a reaction occurs, the same number of electrons came out of the right- and left-hand sides. This was not true with the K-meson. Lee and Yang saw that the K-meson sometimes decayed into two particles and other times into three particles. They went to Chien-Shiung for help. They also read hundreds of pages on the subject and found that there was more than enough mathematical proof for the law of parity. However, no one had done an experiment to back up the mathematical equations. They concluded that there wasn't enough evidence to support or refute parity. They wrote a paper and gave examples of experiments that could be done to prove or disprove the law.

RISING TO THE CHALLENGE

The experiments were too difficult to do and no one was very interested in the project. "Nobody believed it would happen and, because it was so difficult, they wouldn't tackle it. But Chien-Shiung had the perception that right-left symmetry was so basic and fundamental that it should be tested. Even if the experiment had showed it was symmetrical, it would still have been a most important experiment," Yang said, according to *Nobel Prize Women in Science*.

Even Chien-Shiung herself didn't believe she would ever disprove the law of parity. But she was interested in taking on the task of answering a very important question about a basic law of physics. She hadn't been this excited about a project since beta decay. She wanted to start right away.

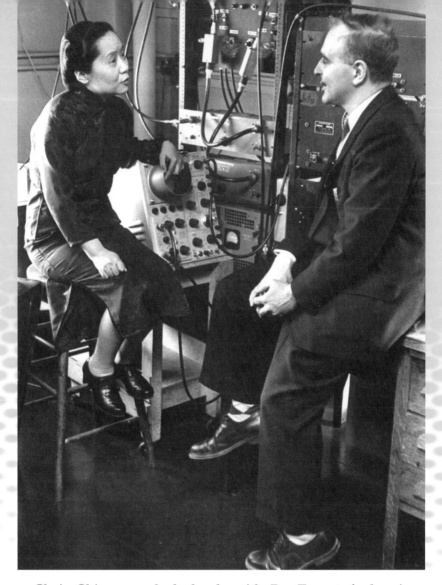

Chein-Shiung worked closely with Dr. Ernest Amber in 1957 during their law of parity experiment. They, along with a group of scientists, worked long hours for a period of six months to prove that the law of parity, a fundamental law of physics, was untrue.

Chien-Shiung and Luke were about to celebrate the twentieth anniversary of the year they left China. They planned a cruise to Europe on the *Queen Elizabeth* where they were to attend a physics conference in Geneva before heading to Asia for a lecture tour. Chien-Shiung didn't want to waste any time or give other scientists the opportunity the get the answer first. Luke went on the trip alone, and Chien-Shiung went to work on the experiment.

Testing Lee and Yang's hypothesis was not easy. Today, conducting such an experiment using advanced computers and machinery would be difficult. The technology available to Chien-Shiung and other scientists in the 1950s was not as accurate, fast, or easy to work with as the technology of today. Chien-Shiung designed an experiment that was very complex.

The nuclei of atoms move very fast in every direction. While they move, heat energy is produced. Chien-Shiung wanted to see if the atoms' nuclei ejected electrons in one direction. If they did, the law of parity would be disproved. In order to study the electrons, Chien-Shiung had to get rid of much of the heat energy. She chose the material she would use very carefully and settled on cobalt 60. Cobalt was a good material because it could be cooled to more than −400 degrees Celsius. At this temperature the nuclei slowed so much they were barely moving. Then a very powerful magnet would be used to force the nuclei to line up. The nuclei would continue to react and emit electrons. Chien-Shiung hoped they would hold still long enough for her to see if the electrons were emitted in one direction.

PUTTING TOGETHER A TEAM

Chien-Shiung had to find a lab that could cool cobalt 60 to the proper temperature. She settled on the National Bureau of Standards in Washington, D.C., which had a cryogenics laboratory, a place where scientists use special refrigeration machines to study physics at low temperatures. There, she put together a team of well-known and well-respected scientists that included Ernest Ambler, Raymond W. Hayward, R. P. Hudson, and D. D. Hoppes.

The team worked day and night for a grueling six months. Chien-Shiung continued to teach at Columbia University in New York City and join her teammates in Washington, D.C., for a few days every two weeks. She got very little sleep as she raced back and forth between the two cities. The other scientists worked around the clock as well. Hoppes slept in a sleeping bag by the equipment. Chien-Shiung's graduate student, Marion Biavati, created the crystals needed for the experiment in a beaker at the same time that she cooked dinner. The team set out to understand a law of physics that had been taken as fact for the past thirty years. They weren't about to miss their chance at a great discovery.

Chien-Shiung was clearly in charge of the team. Although she could not stay in Washington, D.C., for very long periods of time, she expected the best from her coworkers. Her old nickname "the Dragon Lady" came back to haunt her because she

Whether teaching, lecturing, or working in the laboratory, Chien-Shiung gave everything she did her all. She was known for expecting other people, especially students, to work as hard as she did, even if that meant working long hours without a break. Her methods were tough, but effective.

was very serious and hardworking for the duration of the experiment. The other team members liked to play bridge during their lunchtime. But Chien-Shiung did not consider lunchtime an event, only a hassle that took time away from the project.

She worked hard. She didn't let the grueling hours get her down. Chien-Shiung had overcome so much since her early childhood in China. She fought to attend school because she was female.

She fought to get her Ph.D. because she was an Asian woman. She fought for positions at top universities, and she fought for respect once she became a professor. Now she had the opportunity to challenge a fundamental law of physics. She fought for that opportunity. Everything that had come before—the very struggle to succeed—culminated in this experiment.

5

Pollinating the World

On January 9, 1957, every-thing changed for the team. Finally the results were in. Chien-Shiung and her coworkers recorded the direction that each of the released electrons traveled. They called them either "left-handed" or "right-handed," depending on the way they spun out of the nucleus. They found that most of the tens of thousands of electrons emitted by the cobalt nucleus every second were ejected primarily in one direction. This meant that the law of parity was not true in every case. Sometimes the nuclei did not behave symmetrically. Thanks to their work, physicists realized that the law of parity not being observed was the basic property of a single force, now called the weak interaction—one of the four basic forces in the universe. The work was often called the "Wu experiment."

The team celebrated with champagne in the wee hours of the morning. But they could not relax for long. News quickly spread about their discovery. Within days, scientists conducted experiments at Columbia University and confirmed that the result was correct. Other teams of scientists soon proved the law of parity did not hold for other subatomic particles.

Chien-Shiung and her colleagues rushed to get their paper published first. They did beat out the competitors, and Chien-Shiung's name was listed first in the list of scientists in the article that appeared in *Physical Review*, a physics journal. Only the most important scientific papers are published each year in journals. Chien-Shiung's experiment was one of them. Her name being listed first was an honor and show of respect for all of her hard work and leadership. Even so, forty years after the original article was published, an article appeared in *Nature* (another journal) saying that although the

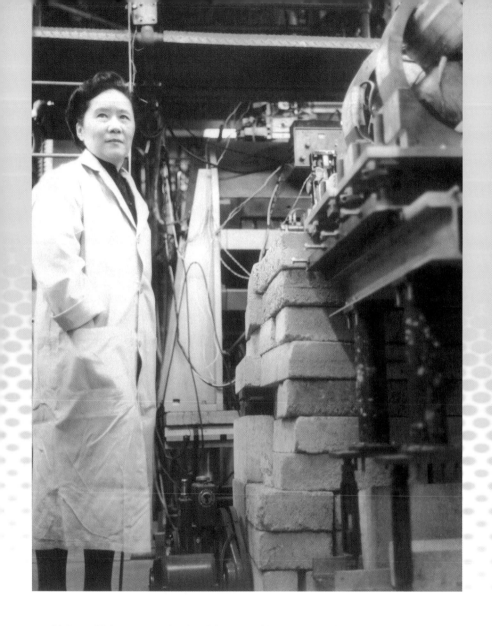

Chien-Shiung worked with complicated machinery to help her scientific research. Here in 1963, she poses with the apparatus that was used to test the weak interaction of subatomic particles.

parity experiment was a team effort, Chien-Shiung's name was listed first only because she was a woman. It seems that even forty years later, Chien-Shiung was still battling discrimination.

A TIME TO CELEBRATE

The team's discovery rocked the physics world. Chien-Shiung's role was especially celebrated. In 1957, an article in the *New York Post* summed up what people around the world thought: "This small, modest woman was powerful enough to do what armies can never accomplish: She helped destroy a law of nature. And laws of nature, by their very definition, should be constant, continuous, immutable, indestructible."

Chien-Shiung, Lee, and Yang were on the cover of magazines across the country. They were interviewed all over the world. Chien-Shiung celebrated the highlight of her postwar career in style. She was honored in every country she visited and gained worldwide recognition as an outstanding physicist. She thought she had reached the peak of her scientific career.

THE NOBEL PRIZE

At the end of the year the Nobel Prizes were to be announced. The Nobel Prizes are international awards given for peace, literature, economics, physics, chemistry, and physiology or medicine. In order to win a science award, a person or group of people have to be nominated by other scientists. In 1957, Lee and Yang won the Nobel Prize for physics. Surprisingly, Chien-Shiung did not share the prize.

Many physicists thought it was unfair that Chien-Shiung did not receive the Nobel Prize for her efforts. Although Lee and Yang originated the idea that the law of parity did not apply universally, Chien-Shiung designed the experiment to test it. There was other competition in the field. A scientist at the University of Chicago had started experimenting at the same time as Chien-Shiung. When her team learned the results of their work, other scientists rushed to find the same answers before Chien-Shiung published them. Nevertheless, Chien-Shiung could not help but feel disappointed because she was not honored with the Nobel Prize.

Clare Boothe Luce, a former U.S. ambassador to Italy and congresswoman, said at the time, "When Dr. Wu knocked out that principle of parity, she established the principle of parity between men and women," according to an article in the *New York Times*, printed on February 18, 1997.

What Luce meant was that discrimination against women was still present. No one can prove that Chien-Shiung did not receive a Nobel Prize because she was a woman. But it is agreed that her work made it possible for Lee and Yang to be so honored. Chien-Shiung, however, did not lose her love of physics just because she failed to win a major international award. She remained committed to the fair treatment of women and their important role in science.

"Bringing a womanly point of view may be advantageous in some areas of education and social science," Chien-Shiung said years later at a conference, according to *Nobel Prize Women in Science*, "but not in physical and mathematical sciences, where we strive always for objectivity. I

Chien-Shiung's time in the laboratory was rewarded with numerous awards and honors. In 1964, one year after this photo was taken, she became the first woman to be presented with the Comstock Award from the National Academy of Sciences.

wonder whether the tiny atoms and nuclei, or the mathematical symbols, or the DNA molecules have any preference for either masculine or feminine treatment."

RECOGNITION COMES

Chien-Shiung did not remain empty-handed for long. Just one year later, in 1958, she became a member of the National Academy of Sciences. She became the first woman to win the Research Corporation Award. Also in that year, she became the first woman to receive an honorary doctorate from Princeton University—the school at which she gained her first position more than a decade earlier. An honorary doctorate is a degree given to people to recognize their outstanding achievements in their field, even if they have not earned that degree by taking classes and tests at the university that issues it.

In the years that followed, Chien-Shung received more awards and much recognition for her work. In 1964, she became the first woman to receive the Comstock Award from the National Academy of Sciences, a prize given out only once every five years. Her fellow physicists named her the first female president of the American Physical Society in 1973. She was given the Scientist of the Year Award by *Industrial Research* magazine in 1974. Israel honored her in 1978 when she won the first Wolf Prize, given to outstanding living scientists and artists, regardless of nationality, race,

CHIEN-SHIUNG WU'S HONORARY DOCTORATES

Receiving an honorary degree is a rare achievement earned by people who excel in their fields. Chien-Shiung Wu had such an incredible impact on the science world that universities practically lined up to honor her. In all, Chien-Shiung received ten honorary doctorates from universities around the country.

- Princeton University (1958)
- Smith College (1959)
- Goucher College (1960)
- Rutgers University (1961)
- Yale University (1967)
- Russell Sage College (1971)
- Harvard University (1974)
- Bard College (1974)
- Adelphi University (1974)
- Dickinson College (1975)

On June 13, 1974, Chien-Shiung received an honorary degree from Harvard University. Each year, only a chosen few are presented with this great honor.

By the end of her career, Chien-Shiung was presented with many prestigious awards and honors. In 1994, both she and her husband Luke (second from right) were presented with the Distinguished Achievement Award from the National Association of Chinese Americans.

color, religion, sex, or political views, for achievements in the interest of mankind and friendly relations among peoples. Chien-Shiung was also given ten honorary degrees from top universities across the United States, including Yale University in New Haven, Connecticut, and Harvard University in Boston, Massachusetts.

Chien-Shiung, however, was not satisfied with merely resting on her reputation and achievements. She knew she had done a great service for the world of physics by helping to prove that the law of parity did not apply to all situations. The physics community gave her

many awards to show their thanks and respect. It was an accepted belief that Chien-Shiung was a major force in the physics community. She was well respected and thought to be at the top of her field. But Chien-Shiung did not conduct research and teach classes to receive awards. She truly loved physics—a subject she would never have studied had it not been for the encouragement of her father and a few textbooks he brought home one summer.

6

A Mind in Full Bloom

Chien-Shiung became a tenured professor at Columbia while continuing to teach. This means she was appointed to her position for life and could not be dismissed from her job unless she committed a serious crime. Chien-Shiung also researched many important topics that helped advance the field of physics. In 1959, two scientists, Richard Feynman and Murray Gell-Mann of the California Institute of Technology, went to Chien-Shiung with a problem, just as Yang and Lee had done. It involved beta decay, the process Chien-Shiung once called "a dear old friend." Feynman and Gell-Man proposed a new law of nature, but Chien-Shiung was too busy to work on this theory. It was not until four years later that she devised another brilliant experiment and proved the proposed law, which was called the conservation of vector current. Once again, Chien-Shiung helped two young men with an idea through her impressive experimental skills. Two years later she wrote *Beta Decay*, which is still a standard reference book for people studying physics.

Chien-Shiung's glory was not entirely without sadness. In 1973, she was finally allowed to visit China. Instead of being greeted by the open arms of her family to celebrate her success, Chien-Shiung found a very different homeland. Political unrest had changed the country she left so many years before. Her parents and brothers were no longer alive. One of her brothers had even committed suicide after extreme persecution from the government.

She returned to the United States very upset about the loss. But even though her father and brothers did not live to see her rise to success, she carried them with her as she went on to research and discover great things as a physicist.

From the day she arrived at the University of California at Berkeley, she said she could not find a scientist who could compare to her father. What she didn't realize was that she was one of those scientists. Considered the "First Lady of Physics," Chien-Shiung was the top-tier scientist her father had dreamed she would be.

TURNING TO MEDICAL RESEARCH

Chien-Shiung continued to research topics that would help people all over the world. She moved into medical research and studied sickle-cell anemia, a disease involving abnormally shaped red blood cells. The cells in healthy people are round, but in people with this disease they become crescent-shaped and have difficulty moving through the body. Sickle-cell anemia patients can experience pain when the abnormally shaped cells block blood vessels. The disease can be fatal.

Eight out of every 100,000 people have sickle-cell anemia. The incidence is even higher among African Americans and Hispanic Americans.

Chien-Shiung's work helped to advance the study of the disease.

Chien-Shiung continued to work at Columbia University. In 1973, she became the first Pupin Professor of Physics. This was an honorary, fully funded position that Chien-Shiung could hold for as long as she wanted. She and Luke lived in an apartment on Claremont Avenue in New York City—a place they would call home for more than fifty years. She retired from the university in 1981. Her old colleagues and Nobel Prize winners Lee and Yang attended her retirement party. She remained friends with both of them many decades after the law of parity experiment.

After she left Columbia University, Chien-Shiung traveled and lectured. She did not forget about her roots. She had received the Chi-Tsin Achievement Award from the Chi-Tsin Culture Foundation in Taiwan in 1965. She returned to both Taiwan and China to teach scientists and advise physics departments in universities across both countries. By then, Taiwan was no longer under the control of China, as it had been before World War II. It was a separate country with its own government. She was awarded honorary professorships from Nanking University, Science and Technology University, Beijing University, Tsao Hwa University, and Nan Kai University.

A STRONG WOMEN'S ADVOCATE

Chien-Shiung returned to the United States and remained a strong advocate of women pursuing careers in science and technology. She was a shining example of what a woman could accomplish when given the opportunity to succeed. Chien-Shiung wanted to make sure other aspiring women were not held back because of their gender. She hoped there would be a time when women were treated as equals to men.

But have things changed since Chien-Shiung was born in 1912? Has discrimination against women been obliterated in the United States—the country that allowed Chien-Shiung to challenge a force of nature? Are women encouraged to study math and science as much as men are?

These are hard questions to answer. Without a doubt, women are filling up seats in science and math classrooms, pages of scientific journals, and spots on scientific award stages throughout the world. The world Chien-Shiung's father imagined, "where every girl [has] a school to go to," may have arrived. Chien-Shiung herself was able to see a drastic change in the treatment of women in science-related fields during her lifetime.

WOMEN WHO HAVE WON THE NOBEL PRIZE IN SCIENCE

Chien-Shiung Wu did not win the Nobel Prize in science. However, ten women have won the prestigious award since 1901. By comparison, about 300 men have won the award.

Continued on p. 92

Continued from p. 91

Marie Curie was not only the first woman to win a Nobel Prize, but she was also the first person to ever win the award twice. Even while battling poverty and discrimination because she was a Polish woman, Curie discovered radium. In 1903, her discovery of radioactivity earned her the Nobel Prize in physics. In 1911, she won the Nobel Prize in chemistry.

Irene Joliot-Curie was the daughter of Marie Curie. She furthered her mother's work in radioactivity. In 1935, she won the Nobel Prize in Chemistry for discovering that radioactivity could be produced artificially.

Gerty Radnitz Cori fought discrimination because she was a Jewish woman. She studied enzymes and hormones. Her work enabled researchers to better understand diabetes. In 1947, she became the first American woman to win the Nobel Prize in biochemistry for discovering the enzymes that convert glycogen into sugar and back again to glycogen.

Barbara McClintock won the Nobel Prize in medicine in 1983. By studying the chromosomes in corn, she discovered antibiotic-resistant bacteria and a possible cure for African sleeping sickness.

Maria Goeppert Mayer researched the structure of the nuclei of atoms. During World War II, she worked on isotope separation for the Manhattan Project. She won the Nobel Prize in physics in 1963. Ten years later, she was finally able to achieve a paid position at a university.

Rita Levi-Montalcini started her work in her tiny bedroom after the government of Italy

forbade Jews from practicing medicine or studying science during World War II. In 1954, she discovered a nerve growth factor—a protein that stimulates the growth of nerve cells. The factor also

Continued on p. 94

Continued from p. 93

plays a role in diseases like Alzheimer's disease. She received the Nobel Prize in medicine in 1986.

Dorothy Crowfoot Hodgkin discovered the structures of penicillin and vitamin B-12 using X-ray analysis. She won the Nobel Prize in chemistry in 1964 for determining the structure of biochemical compounds needed to combat pernicious anemia, or vitamin B-12 deficiency. Hodgkin waged her own battles. She fought debilitating arthritis and was discriminated against because she had ties to Communism.

Gertrude Elion realized that because she was a woman she had to work twice as hard as a man to get a

chemistry job during the Great Depression. She is the only woman inventor inducted into the Inventors Hall of Fame. She invented a drug that helps fight leukemia and won the

Nobel Prize in medicine and physiology in 1988. Later she also invented a drug that blocks the body's rejection of foreign tissues during transplant operations.

Rosalyn Sussman Yalow won the Nobel Prize in medicine in 1977. Neither of her parents finished high school, but Yalow was determined to get an education and succeed, despite the discrimination she received being a Jewish woman. She and her partner, Solomon A. Berson, developed radio immunoassay (RIA), a test of body tissues that measures the concentrations of hormones, viruses, vitamins, enzymes, and drugs. RIA revolutionized the treatment of diseases like diabetes that are caused by hormonal problems. She was awarded the Nobel Prize after Berson's death.

Christiane Nüsslein-Volhard won the Nobel Prize in medicine in 1995. She helped explain how a single cell becomes a complex creature. She and her partner, Eric Wieschaus, also used the fruit fly to help explain birth defects in humans.

THE LEGACY OF CHIEN-SHIUNG WU

When she died after a second stroke (about two years after her first) on February 16, 1997, at the age of eighty-four, Chien-Shiung left a legacy. She was the first woman to become an instructor in the physics department of Princeton University; the first woman to receive an honorary degree from Princeton University; the first woman to be elected president of the American Physical Society; and the first woman to receive the Comstock Award. In 1990, an asteroid was named after her. This was the first time an asteroid had been named for a living scientist.

"She was the world's distinguished woman physicist of her time," said William Havens, a Columbia University professor emeritus of applied physics and nuclear engineering in Chien-Shiung's *New York Times* obituary, printed on February 18, 1997.

Her son, Vincent Yuan, continued the family tradition. He became a respected physicist in his own right. He works at Los Alamos Laboratory in

New Mexico—the site where much of the work on the Manhattan Project was done.

Chien-Shiung's tradition continues in other ways. Throughout the world, young students continue to learn about the advancements she made in physics. The Chinese government set up an educational foundation in her name to promote scientific education. In Shitou, China, the foundation runs the Wu Chien-Shiung Science Camp for high school and college students who are gifted in chemistry, physics, and biology. Over 100 students from many countries come to the camp to learn from accomplished scientists.

In 1992, China opened a public laboratory bearing Chien-Shiung's name to recognize her phenomenal achievements. The Chien-Shiung Wu Laboratory is located in Nanjing, the city where Chien-Shiung attended the National Central University. The laboratory had been proposed nine years earlier by Yu Wei, a distinguished female electronic engineering scientist who saw Chien-Shiung as a role model.

AN INSPIRING LIFE

Chien-Shiung Wu was told that she couldn't go to school because she was a girl. She was told that she couldn't help do research for the war effort because she was a woman. She was told that she couldn't become a university professor until the male professors left their positions. She was told that she couldn't win the world's top physics prizes. For much of her life, she was told that she couldn't. But she did.

Chien-Shiung didn't stop there. She went on to encourage other women to study science and find careers in it, just as her father had encouraged her so many years before. She was a flower in the desert. Chien-Shiung did not have everything she needed to thrive. She faced discrimination because of her gender and race. Nevertheless, she put down her roots and spread her leaves despite this unfairness. She was able to succeed because of her determination, hard work, and bravery.

In her lifetime Chien-Shiung Wu overcame many obstacles and achieved greatness in the world of physics. Her contributions to science will not soon be forgotten.

"It is the courage to doubt what has long been established, the incessant search for its verification and proof that pushed the wheel of science forward," Chien-Shiung said, according to *American Women Scientists*. Chien-Shiung Wu was truly a courageous hero.

TIMELINE

1912	Chien-Shiung Wu is born on May 31 in Shanghai, China.
1921	Chien-Shiung graduates from her father's school and begins studying at the Soochow Girls' School.
1936	After graduating from the National Central University in Nanjing, Chien-Shiung goes to the United States.
1940	Chien-Shiung earns her Ph.D. from the University of California, Berkeley.
1942	During the summer, Chien-Shiung marries Luke Yuan at the home of Robert Millikan.
1943	Chien-Shiung becomes the first female instructor at Princeton University.
1947	Chien-Shiung gives birth to her son, Vincent Yuan.
1957	Chien-Shiung helps disprove the law of parity.

1958	Chien-Shiung is elected as a member of the National Academy of Sciences, receives the Research Corporation Award, and becomes the first woman to receive an honorary doctorate from Princeton University.
1963	Chien-Shiung proves the conservation of vector current law.
1964	Chien-Shiung receives the Comstock Award from the National Academy of Sciences.
1975	Chien-Shiung receives the National Medal of Science and becomes the first female president of the American Physical Society.
1978	Chien-Shiung becomes the first person to win the Wolf Prize in Physics from Israel.
1981	Chien-Shiung retires from Columbia University.
1990	An asteroid is named after Chien-Shiung.
1997	Chien-Shiung Wu dies on February 16 at the age of eighty-four.

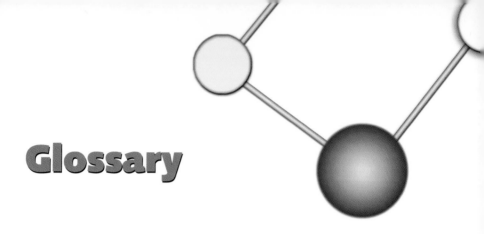

Glossary

accelerator A machine used to smash atoms into pieces.

atom The building block of all matter, made of protons, neutrons, and electrons.

beta decay A type of radioactivity in which an atom's nucleus ejects certain parts and then changes into another element.

boycott The act of refusing to purchase or utilize a group of products or services.

civil war A war between different groups in the same country.

chain reaction A series of events, each of which is started by the one before it.

Communism The system of government that believes that property should be shared among an entire population.

cyclotron A machine developed by Ernest Lawrence that smashed atoms together at very high speeds.

democracy A type of government in which people are voted into power by citizens.

discrimination The act of treating a person differently because of his or her race, sex, religion, or class.

dynasty A succession of rulers from the same family who are born into power.

fission Splitting an atom's nucleus to release energy.

fusion The process of fusing two atoms together, producing less energy than fission.

nuclear energy The energy released when the nucleus of an atom splits or is fused with another atom's nucleus.

nucleus The center of an atom.

physics The study of energy, matter, and motion.

radiation The process of emitting waves or particles of energy.

revolutionary A person who works toward political or social change.

subatomic particles Pieces of an atom that exist for only a few seconds during a reaction.

For More Information

The American Physical Society
One Physics Ellipse
College Park, MD 20740-3844
(301) 209-3200
Web site: http://www.aps.org

The National Academy of Sciences
500 Fifth Street NW
Washington, DC 20001
(202) 334-2000
Web site: http://www4.nationalacademies.org/nas

The National Science Foundation
4201 Wilson Boulevard
Arlington, VA 22230
(800) 877-8339
Web site: http://www.nsf.gov

The National Women's Hall of Fame

76 Fall Street

P.O. Box 335

Seneca Falls, NY 13148

(315) 568-8060

Web site: http://www.greatwomen.org

WEB SITES

Due to the changing nature of Internet links, the Rosen Publishing Group, Inc., has developed an online list of Web sites related to the subject of this book. This site is updated regularly. Please use this link to access the list:

http://www.rosenlinks.com/whof/whfms/cswu/

For Further Reading

Howes, Ruth H., and Caroline L. Herzenberg. *Their Day in the Sun: Women of the Manhattan Project*. Philadelphia: Temple University Press, 1999.

McGrayne, Sharon Bertsch. *Nobel Prize Women in Science: Their Lives, Struggles, and Momentous Discoveries*. Secaucus, NJ: Carol Publishing Group, 1998.

Reynolds, Moira Davison. *American Women Scientists: 23 Inspiring Biographies, 1900–2000*. Jefferson, NC: McFarland & Company, Incorporated Publishers, 1999.

Stille, Darlene R. *Extraordinary Women Scientists*. Chicago: Chicago Children's Press, 1995.

Bibliography

Dicke, William. "Chien-Shiung Wu, 84, Top Experimental Physicist." *New York Times,* February 18, 1997.

Howes, Ruth H., and Caroline L. Herzenberg. *Their Day in the Sun: Women of the Manhattan Project.* Philadelphia: Temple University Press, 1999.

Mei-chun, Lin. "First Lady of Chinese Physics Honored." *Taipei Times*, August 16, 2000.

McGrayne, Sharon Bertsch. *Nobel Prize Women in Science: Their Lives, Struggles, and Momentous Discoveries.* Secaucus, NJ: Carol Publishing Group, 1998.

Nelson, Bob. "Famed Physicist Chien-Shiung Wu Dies at 84." *Columbia University Record*, February 21, 1997, Vol. 22, No. 15.

Newman, H. B., and T. Ypsilantis. *History of Original Ideas and Basic Discoveries in Particle Physics*. New York: Plenum Publishing Company, 1996.

Reynolds, Moira Davison. *American Women Scientists: 23 Inspiring Biographies, 1900–2000*. Jefferson, NC: McFarland & Company, Incorporated Publishers, 1999.

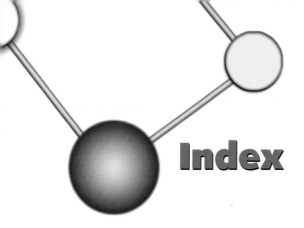

Index

ABOUT THE AUTHOR

Stephanie H. Cooperman, a graduate of the University of Pennsylvania, is currently employed at a large book publishing company. She is a writer who freelances for both print and Web site publications. She is very interested in science-related topics and was fascinated by Chien-Shiung Wu's story, particularly Wu's "old friend," beta decay. She thinks all women should be encouraged to study math and science. She lives in New York City.

DESIGN AND LAYOUT

Evelyn Horovicz

EDITOR

Eliza Berkowitz